IS THAT NORMAL?

A Pediatrician's Guide
for Parents of Newborns

MEGHAN BURKE, MD

with Illustrations by Glenn Sarsale

Print ISBN: 979-8-35093-425-0

eBook ISBN: 979-8-35093-426-7

INTRODUCTION

Is that normal? As a pediatrician, this is one of the most common questions I am asked by parents about their children.

Specifically, from parents of newborns, the question is usually preceded by a variety of observations and concerns they have about their newborns. For me, newborns are second nature. But for parents, particularly first-timers, every noise or movement, every rash or skin imperfection, and every poop or lack of poop triggers anxiety and frantic internet searches. According to the internet, your baby is one step away from turning into a lizard with ten eyeballs. According to me, your baby is completely normal.

Whether it is your first or fourth time around, the newborn period (the first four weeks of life) can be the most exhilarating time of your life while simultaneously being the most stressful. The stress is due in large part to the unknown. This book (not the internet) is intended to serve as a quick and valid guidebook to help with the unknown. I like to reassure parents that the hardest part of being a newborn is the brief transition from the womb to the outside world. Once they are here, very few things can go wrong. So, don't worry, you got this.

I wrote this book with the advantage of being on both sides of the fence: a former nervous new mom and a pediatrician. When I was a first time parent to my newborn son, I had already been a practicing pediatrician for eight years. During my maternity leave, you'd think I never even went to medical school much less trained as a pediatrician. I couldn't figure out breastfeeding, I was obsessed with my son's poop, I overanalyzed every move he made, and I went through some pretty rough postpartum depression. What helped me tremendously was our son's second visit to the pediatrician's office. I saw a nurse practitioner who spent ten percent of the visit on my perfectly healthy newborn and ninety percent on me. She saw that I was struggling despite my efforts to put on a happy face. She made me realize that the most important part of the first few weeks in a newborn's life is making sure the parents are adjusting. With that in mind, and having so many parents say they wished there were a handbook for newborn care; this is what I came up with. I really hope it helps.

Disclaimer: The information contained in this book is for educational purposes only and should not substitute for medical care from your pediatrician.

To my family Glenn, Jack, and Murphy – this book is for you.

ACKNOWLEDGMENTS

Many thanks to the following people who helped with editing:

NAILAH - my bestie in the westie, the most accomplished doctor I may ever know.

COURTNEY - CPNP extraordinaire, my pretzel and cheese champion.

SARAH - my rock through medical school and residency.

HELEN – my honorary sister.

AMANDA - my amazing, and crazy-in-a-good-way cousin.

CONTENTS

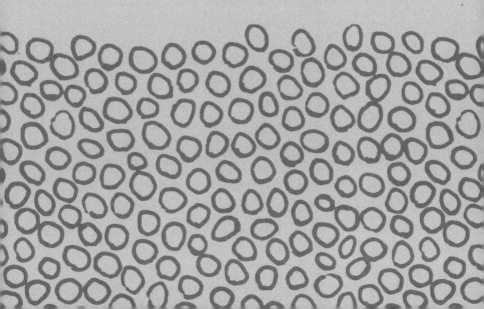

"It seems like she wants to feed
all the time. Is that normal?"

FEEDING

Newborns feed frequently. Some days it will feel like your baby is feeding every five minutes. At some point during the first few days of life, most newborns will do something known as cluster feeding, where they concentrate their feeds into back-to-back sessions. This most often occurs throughout the night and early morning hours. It goes something like this: it's 3:30 am, you just fed your newborn, changed their diaper, climb back into bed, and twenty minutes later they wake to feed again. Definitely feed them and definitely don't worry, as cluster feeding is short-lived (a few days/nights at most) and will stop.

Overall, you will want to ensure eight to twelve feeds (breast or formula) in a twenty-four-hour period. When you do the math, that's feeding every two to three hours. If you are breastfeeding, nursing this frequently not only keeps your baby fed but also stimulates your breasts to amp up your milk supply.

In the first few weeks keep a log of feeds.

Breastfed: How often and for how long.

Bottle-fed: How often and how much (in milliliters or ounces).

A note on the amount (bottle) and time (breast) your baby takes: it is nearly impossible to overfeed a newborn no matter how tiny anyone tells you their stomach is. There is no amount that is too much. Newborns eat when they are hungry and stop when they are full. Regarding breast-fed infants, they can stay on your breast far longer than it takes to get the milk, i.e., they use the breast as a pacifier. If they are continuously sucking for fifteen to twenty minutes on each breast, you can stop them.

Once weight gain has been steady as determined by your pediatrician and you are confident with feeds, you can stop logging. PLEASE stop logging. You will free up time and more importantly, your mind.

Here's a tidbit about breastfeeding: nobody tells you how difficult it can be and that often it doesn't work right away (or ever) because both you and your baby need to learn how to do it. Yes, it's "natural," but so is giving birth, and was that easy? There seems to be an unrealistic expectation that women can simply pop their newborn onto the breast and go skipping through a field of daisies. And while for some it does happen that way, for many others it does not. If you are struggling, lean on friends and family members that breastfed, try a lactation consultant, or talk to your pediatrician for resources. In the end, if it's causing you more distress than joy, it's ok to stop. Again, IT IS OK TO STOP. Breastfeeding is an extremely personal decision for the person to whom the breasts belong.

"Sometimes I can't get him
to burp. Is that normal?"

BURPING

If you've tried to get your baby to burp, and it's been a good three to four minutes and there's still no burp, then there is just no burp to be had. You can stop.

I'll take it a step further, and likely make your own mother's head spin, but there's no rule that you need to burp babies at all. If they need to, they will do it on their own without the back slaps.

"She hasn't pooped in two days. Is that normal?"

POOPING

Get ready to fixate on poop. I'll tell you not to, but it's inevitable. So, here's the scoop on poop. The first poop(s) is thick, black, and sticky. This is called meconium. Over the first few days, the poop should transition to yellow, seedy (it looks like there are sesame seeds mixed in) and runny for breastfed infants. Poop is normally a little thicker for formula-fed infants.

Once your baby's poop transitions from meconium, the following holds true:

FREQUENCY

In the beginning, most newborns poop more than they pee. They can poop during or after every feed. They look at you and they poop. You look at them and they poop. Then after a few weeks, the pooping becomes less frequent. Your baby may go several days without pooping. Consider it a savings on diapers.

EFFORT

Sometime around two weeks old, some babies start to push, strain, and turn red when trying to poop. It no longer slips out effortlessly as it once did. You can help by bending their legs at the knees and gently pressing the legs into the belly This helps to increase pressure in the abdominal cavity to push out the poop. This is a phase and will pass.

COLOR

Any color poop is okay, except black, white, and red (with blood). And yes, that means green poop is normal. Just wait until they eat their first handful of blueberries later on.

CONSTIPATION

Despite the aforementioned straining and/or less frequent poops, it is extremely rare for a newborn to get truly constipated. Provided they are acting and feeding normally, and the poop is liquid or soft, skipping days and straining are a normal part of newborn pooping. If they become abnormally fussy, it's time to call your pediatrician.

"Her pee looked pink this morning. Is that normal?"

PEEING

COLOR – Pink-hued urine, and sometimes even orange, is normal. The color is due to the urine being highly concentrated. After the first few days, the urine should be slightly yellow to almost colorless.

FREQUENCY – As a general rule of thumb, the daily number of wet diapers should match your newborn's age in days. For example, your baby should have at least one wet diaper on day one of life, two on day two, three on day three and so on. Once your milk is in (if breastfeeding) and once the baby's feeding pattern is established, you can expect five or more wet diapers daily by one week of age and going forward. And remember, your "days" are not sunrise to sunset anymore. They are a full twenty-four hours, so those middle-of-the-night wet diapers count.

Once feeding is going well and your baby is gaining weight, you can stop logging the wet diapers.

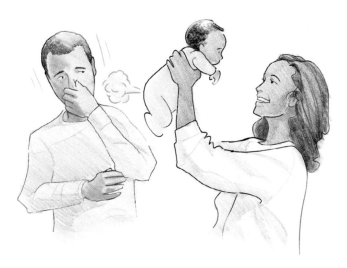

"He's been really gassy
lately. Is that normal?"

GAS

Newborns tend to get increasingly gassy over the first few weeks of life. The gas is loud, it stinks, and worst of all, it can be uncomfortable. But the good news is, it's NORMAL and it will pass (pun intended). If you are breastfeeding, don't automatically blame yourself for what you ate. If you are formula feeding, don't immediately jump to change the formula. Just be patient.

HOW CAN YOU HELP?

MANEUVERS:

- Bend the baby's knees and push both legs into the belly repeatedly. This is different from "bicycling," which is one leg at a time. Pushing both legs simultaneously increases pressure in the abdominal cavity and helps to expel the gas.

- Tummy massage (clockwise) with gentle pressure.

MEDICATIONS:

Over-the-counter gas drops (probiotics and simethicone).

AIR FRESHENER AND A FAN:

As I mentioned, it stinks.

"His skin is peeling.
Is that normal?"

RASHES

Newborns are prone to several different types of rashes. Some of these rashes can be helped with ointments or creams while others just need time to resolve.

●●●●●●●●●●●●

CRACKING/PEELING SKIN:

Newborns can have very dry skin that appears like it's cracking or peeling. Very often this happens around the ankles, around the wrists, and on the abdomen. Repeatedly moisturizing with an unscented cream or ointment (I recommend petroleum jelly) will fix it right up.

●●●●●●●●●●●●

DIAPER RASH:

Most diaper rashes can be cured with any zinc oxide-based diaper cream. When I was a pediatric resident in training, I was taught that if the skin is red, use a white cream (zinc oxide-based) to heal it. And once the rash has cleared, put the clear ointment (petroleum jelly) on to protect it from developing a rash. In short, white on red, clear on clear.

●●●●●●●●●●●●

BABY ACNE:

Typically, around one month, give or take a week, your angel-faced infant can get zits. Yes, zits. You did nothing to cause it, and you can do nothing to make it go away. The process has to do with maternal hormones your baby was exposed to while in utero that are now fading naturally. It will resolve on its own without any intervention needed. Of note, it can also spread to the neck, chest, stomach, and back.

· · · · · · · · · · · ·

ERYTHEMA TOXICUM:

This is the most terrifying name for a rash that is completely benign. It usually starts at any time after the first twenty-four to forty-eight hours of life. It looks like red blotches with a small white bump in the middle. This rash usually resolves within a week.

· · · · · · · · · · · ·

DERMAL MELANOCYTOSIS:

These flat bluish-colored marks occur mostly in babies of Asian, Latin American, and African American descent. They are harmless from a medical perspective. The most common areas to find these spots are on the buttocks, shoulders, and lower back; however, you may see them in other places. Even though they may look like bruises, they are not. The color is due to the incomplete migration of pigment cells up to the skin's surface. They will fade in most kids by age five.

· · · · · · · · · · · ·

NEVUS SIMPLEX (AKA STORK BITE, ANGEL KISSES):

This is a common rash that is red and flat and can be found at the nape of the neck (stork bite), between the eyebrows, or on the eyelids (angel kisses). The stork bite refers to the folktale where storks deliver babies to families while holding the baby by the back of the neck, hence leaving a rash. Angel kisses you can probably figure out. Nevus simplex rash can also be seen under the nose but there's no cute name for that one.

"His umbilical cord is
bleeding. Is that normal?"

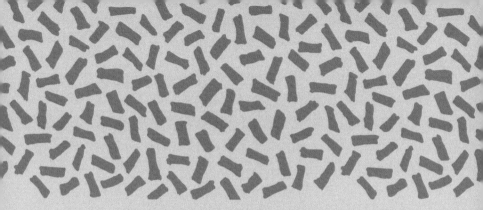

UMBILICAL CORD CARE

I t's normal to see a little bit of blood on the clothing before and after the umbilical stump has fallen off. It should fall off within the first few days to weeks. The only thing you need to do is keep it dry. This is why we advise no bath in a tub until it falls off—water won't harm it; it will just keep it attached longer.

A sponge bath is fine; just avoid the area. You do not need to apply rubbing alcohol to the area. This is an old practice and is unnecessary.

It's also normal for the umbilical stump to have a foul odor. My son's smelled like a dumpster full of rotten fish on a hot summer day. It was gag-worthy.

What's NOT normal is when the area on the abdomen surrounding the stump becomes red and hard. This means the area is infected and needs immediate medical attention. That being said, I have yet to see a single infected umbilical stump in my entire career.

"He hiccups all the time.
Is that normal?"

HICCUPS

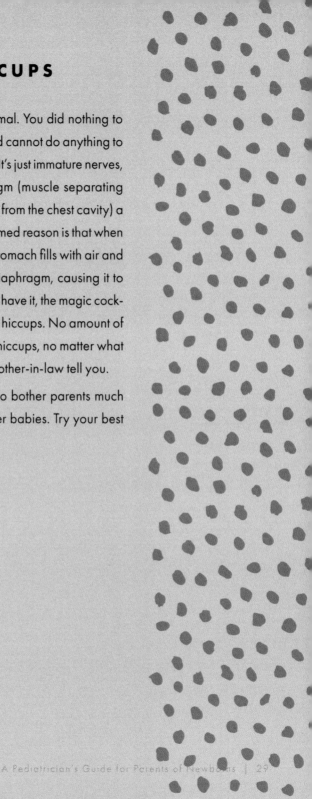

Hiccups are normal. You did nothing to cause them and cannot do anything to make them go away. It's just immature nerves, making the diaphragm (muscle separating the abdominal cavity from the chest cavity) a little jumpy. The presumed reason is that when your baby eats, the stomach fills with air and pushes against the diaphragm, causing it to spasm. And there you have it, the magic cocktail that creates baby hiccups. No amount of burping will prevent hiccups, no matter what your mom and/or mother-in-law tell you.

Hiccups tend to bother parents much more than they bother babies. Try your best to ignore them.

"He was so quiet when we brought him home, and now he is crying a lot. Is that normal?"

CRYING

Here's the deal: babies cry. And just when you think you've figured out why and you fix it, they cry some more.

There is a somewhat predictable timeline to it. Somewhere around two weeks old, babies learn how to cry, like really belt it out. There is often no rhyme or reason. It can be challenging to soothe them, and often you just need to wait until they tire, which can take up to an hour or more. At this point you may be crying too, which is okay. Many infants have a so-called witching hour when the crying tends to peak. This often happens later in the day or evening. These crying episodes usually begin to level off at three to four months old. There is a light at this seemingly endless tunnel, even when it is 2:30am and you haven't slept longer than a three-hour stretch in weeks.

During the newborn period it is not recommended to let your baby cry it out. Do your best to try to comfort them. Various soothing techniques include rocking, singing, feeding, playing calming music, swaddling, or anything else you think may help. However there may be instances where nothing seems to work. In those moments, focus on calming yourself as a crying baby can be quite frustrating. I promise, it WILL get better.

"I think she may have colic. Is that normal? Because it's awful!"

COLIC

Colic is defined using the "rule of three": Crying for more than three hours per day, for more than three days per week, for at least three weeks, in an otherwise healthy infant. What's the cardinal feature of the definition of colic? A lot of crying. So I direct you back to the last section on crying. Is this normal? Yes. Is it awful? Yes. But to reiterate, it will get better.

He's been sneezing a lot.
Is that normal?"

SNEEZING

Sneezing is normal in newborns. They have tiny nasal passages and therefore can get clogged more easily. They sneeze to keep the passages open and clear. Many parents worry that their newborn may have allergies. Newborns are too young for environmental or pet allergies so you can keep your pet!

"I try to swaddle her, but she always wants her arms free. Is that normal?"

SWADDLING

Swaddling can be soothing for newborns as it mimics the compact position in the womb. Regardless of how well you think you wrap them, they can Houdini their little arms out in the blink of an eye. Don't blame your swaddling skills; instead, take credit for the incredible strength you passed down to your child. There's no rule that says you must swaddle a baby.

Discussions about when to no longer swaddle from a safety standpoint can be had with your pediatrician. I recommend stopping either when babies indicate they don't like it, or when they start rolling over, which is usually around four months.

"He seems really congested.
Is that normal?"

CONGESTION

Newborns may sound congested for several reasons: a small amount of amniotic fluid remaining in the nose, floppy nasal cartilage, small nasal passages, and the presence of mucus and milk in the back of the nose and throat. Some or all of these factors can contribute.

The best remedy for congestion is to use infant nasal saline drops (available at any pharmacy over the counter), and then suction the nose with either a bulb syringe or a snot sucker. Bear in mind that the congestion more often bothers parents, not babies. Here's a trick: plug your ears to silence the congestion noises. Look at your baby. If they appear comfortable and undisturbed by the congestion, all is well. If this is the case, the best remedy becomes time to let it pass.

"Sometimes I see him
breathing hard and
fast when he's asleep.
Is that normal?"

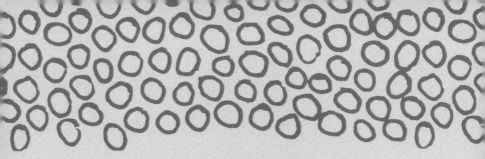

RAPID BREATHING

This normal newborn phenomenon is called periodic breathing. Your baby will take a series of repetitive rapid breaths, followed by a pause of up to ten seconds, and then rapid breaths again. Newborns tend to cycle through periodic breathing during sleep. It is harmless and will resolve within a few months.

"She sleeps a lot. Is that normal?"

SLEEP

In the beginning, all your newborn will do is sleep when they aren't feeding. It's a leisurely life of eating, sleeping, and pooping. Jealous? Me too.

By one to two months old, babies will start to have more awake time. As time goes on, the tables will turn, and your child won't sleep. Or they'll wake all the time to feed or cry, or simply to torture you. Later on, they will demand that you read a fifth book before turning off the lights. Or they will come into your room at 2 am and insist they saw a monster. Fun stuff.

SOME NOTES ON SAFE SLEEPING:

WHERE: Only in a bassinet or a crib with a firm mattress positioned flat, not inclined. There is a big risk in allowing your newborn to sleep in bed with you. You could inadvertently roll over on them and they can suffocate. This is a rare event, but one is too many. Additionally, allowing your newborn to sleep in a swing or any other infant seat carries a risk as well.

HOW: On their back, facing the ceiling. Please refrain from blankets, pillows, stuffed animals, and bumpers. All you want in the crib or bassinet is your baby.

Ensuring all the above can help reduce the risk of sudden infant death syndrome (SIDS). SIDS is the unexplained death in a usually healthy baby less than a year of age, most often during sleep. Please know that SIDS is rare, so it is unlikely this will happen, but ensuring safe sleep is key.

"I heard we should wait at least one week to give her a bath. Is that normal?"

BATHING

The only thing you really need to wait for is the umbilical stump to detach (see section on umbilical cord care). When you put your newborn into the tub, always feel the water first and ensure it is lukewarm, not hot, as an infant's skin is more sensitive to temperature than ours. Before the stump has fallen off, you can still wash them; you will just want to avoid getting the stump wet. Whether you do that in the tub or decide on a sponge bath is up to you.

You can bathe your newborn as frequently or infrequently as you wish. In all honesty, you can tell when it is time for a bath when their scalp starts to be a bit stinky. You'll know what I mean when it happens.

I recommend using a soft washcloth, a gentle sponge, or just your hands with the baby wash of your choice. Moisturizing the skin after a bath is also a good idea.

As a matter of safety, do not leave your infant alone in the water for even one second. And, as a matter of fact, most babies love a bath; so have fun.

"His nails are so long
and he's scratching his
face. Is that normal?"

NAIL CARE

Newborns have very soft fingernails. To prevent them from scratching themselves, I recommend using little mittens or long-sleeved shirts that fold over the hands. You can attempt to file the nails with a traditional nail file, but quite frankly, it doesn't really work. You can also try to clip the nails with lighted baby nail clippers. The best time to try is when your baby is sleeping, so their hands are still. If you inadvertently clip the skin (we all have), don't panic. Will it bleed? Probably. Just apply pressure. Will your baby cry? Probably. Will you cry? DEFINITELY.

But it's okay. The skin will heal, and so will you.

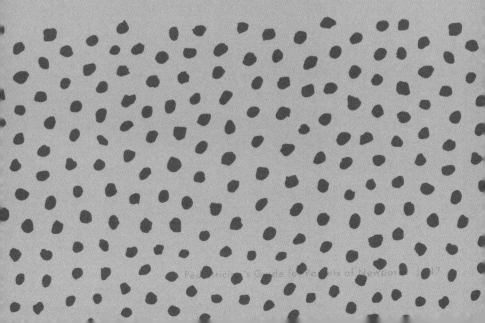

"He was circumcised
and his penis is so red.
Is that normal?"

"She has mucus coming from
her vagina. Is that normal?

GENITAL CARE:

PENIS

Yes, this is very normal. Note the following:

A newly circumcised penis will look bright red and can have yellow material that often is mistaken for pus. It's not; it's normal healing skin. The penis will heal in five to ten days.

Circumcised penis care: Caring for a newly circumcised penis involves nothing more than squeezing out a glob of petroleum jelly onto a piece of gauze and placing it on the tip of the penis with every diaper change. If you are feeling bold, skip the gauze entirely and just apply a generous amount of petroleum jelly directly to the penis. You can stop once the head of the penis returns to the same color as the rest of the penis.

Uncircumcised penis care: An uncircumcised penis needs no special care. You do not need to pull back the foreskin to clean it. In fact, if you leave it alone, it will take care of itself.

VAGINA

Vaginal mucus in a newborn is normal. It is also normal to see some blood. Both are due to maternal hormones and should resolve in about one week.

I am also often asked how to clean the vaginal area during diaper changes. You do not have to go digging in order to clean. After you have wiped, if you still notice some mucus or poop inside the labia, it's okay to leave it there.

"Her head feels all lumpy.
Is that normal?"

SKULL

Newborn skulls are not one uniform bone like ours. Instead, their skulls are composed of several bones with two soft spots (one on top, and a smaller one in back). This design allows for more flexibility of the head to squeeze through the birth canal. Between these different skull pieces, you can sometimes feel bumps, ridges, or valleys. This is normal. The soft spots will eventually close, and the bones will all eventually fuse and feel more uniform. No one has a perfectly round head. You have probably never done this, but feel your own head. I guarantee you will find a bump or two.

"He won't take a pacifier.
Is that normal?"

PACIFIERS

Some babies take them, some don't. Some parents use them from day one, others are wholly opposed to them. If you want to use a pacifier, I say go for it, but I recommend waiting until you have the feeding routine established and you know your baby is gaining weight. The American Academy of Pediatrics recommends waiting at least four weeks. However, you can make your own decision on this one. You are likely to get a different opinion from everyone you ask, including your pediatrician, so try not to overthink it.

"She spits up after every
feed. Is that normal?"

SPIT-UP

Spitting up is a common and normal occurrence in babies. As long as it's not green, bloody, projectile, or seemingly painful, you are in the clear. And by projectile, I mean it's hitting the wall on the opposite side of the room.

Remember, spit-up is most often a laundry problem, not a medical one. As long as your baby is content and gaining weight, there is no intervention needed.

"Her eyes have yellow
goo coming from them.
Is that normal?"

GOOPY EYES

In newborns, goopy eyes are most commonly a result of clogged tear ducts (aka nasolacrimal duct stenosis), which is a normal newborn phenomenon. Tear ducts are located at the inner corner of the lower eyelid and drain tears. Therefore, clogged tear ducts cause excess tearing and/or yellow mucus from one or both eyes. This almost always spontaneously resolves and can take up to one year of age to do so. It can also come and go. You can gently wipe away the goo with a soft cloth or a cotton ball, moistened with warm water. To help open the tear ducts, you can gently massage the side of the nose right under the affected eye in a downward motion (away from the eye). Whether or not you choose to massage, the duct should eventually open.

"I've noticed her eyes
sometimes cross. Is
that normal?"

VISION AND CROSSED EYES

Crossed eyes are a normal newborn occurrence because they lack the eye muscle control to focus on an object. This usually resolves at two to three months. However, if just one eye seems to be floating inward or outward, inform your pediatrician.

Newborns cannot see past eight to twelve inches. Get up close and personal as often as possible so they can see you. As time goes on, they will be able to see greater distances. The first time they are able to see you walk into a room and they smile, your heart will melt.

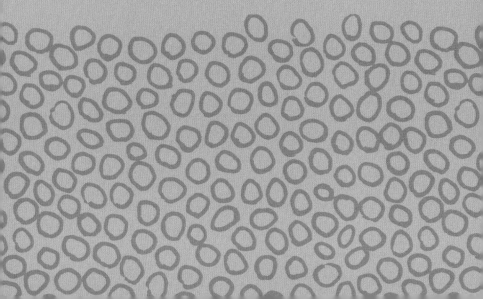

"I heard newborns always need
to wear a hat. Is that normal?"

DRESSING BABY

This is simple. Dress your baby as you would dress in any temperature or weather condition plus one extra layer. Be sure to always have extra layers should you need them. And despite what your parents tell you, your infant does not need a hat when indoors. They will not "lose all of their heat" through their heads. In fact, the American Academy of Pediatrics recommends against hats while indoors, particularly while sleeping, as they can be unsafe.

"I heard I can't take him out until he gets his first vaccines. Is that true?"

TAKING BABY OUT/
HAVING VISITORS

Absolutely not. Please do not coop yourself up at home. If the weather permits, go out, take a walk, and get some fresh air. I would recommend that you avoid very crowded places for prolonged periods of time, as there is more risk for contracting illnesses like the common cold.

Can you go out with your newborn to Target? Yes. Should you go to a kid's birthday party at a bounce house? Nope.

If friends and family want to visit, make sure they are not sick, and have them wash their hands prior to holding your baby. And now that COVID is here to stay, I recommend visitors wear a mask, but I will leave that one up to you.

"He feels hot all the time.
Does he have a fever?"

FEVER

The answer is: very unlikely. Newborns emit a lot of heat. They can have sweaty heads and backs. However, if your baby feels hotter than usual, take their temperature.

Fever = 100.4°F or higher, taken rectally (the preferred method for newborns)

If an infant from birth to two months has a fever, go to the closest emergency department, preferably at a pediatric hospital if there is one close by.

Do not take your infant's temperature "just to check." It is uncommon for newborns to have a fever, but if they do, you will know. Fevers are not subtle- they feel HOT, not warm, but HOT.

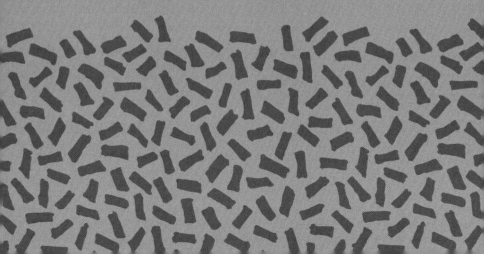

"I'm scared I am going to break her when I change her? Is that normal?"

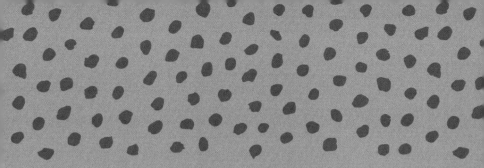

YOU WILL NOT BREAK
YOUR BABY

It is very normal for parents to think their newborn is as fragile as glass. It can take many parents close to five full minutes to undress their baby when they first come into my office for the newborn visit. By the fifth visit, they can do it with eyes closed, one hand, and in less than five seconds. Infants are very sturdy and stronger than you think. Just handle with care and definitely remember to support their neck when you are carrying them, as it's common for them to throw their heads back spontaneously. But rest assured, you will not break your baby if you have to hold back a leg while changing a diaper, or gently shove an unbending arm into a sleeve. This is just your reassurance piece and with practice you will gain confidence.

"My friend is splitting up the vaccines for her baby. Is that a normal thing to do?"

VACCINES

Not only is it not normal but it is also ill-informed and frankly, dangerous.

Please do not think twice about whether to vaccinate your child. Vaccines are safe. Vaccines are effective. Do not split up the vaccines, do not follow any of the many "alternative" schedules found online, and do not come up with your own schedule. Follow the vaccination schedule that we know works and is supported by the Centers for Disease Control (CDC) and the American Academy of Pediatrics (AAP).

As pediatricians, our primary objective is to safeguard your baby's health. Vaccines play a crucial role in achieving this goal, providing protection for your baby and contributing to the overall safety of society against severe and potentially life-threatening diseases.

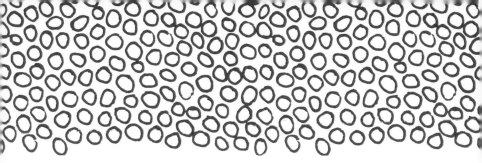

"I've been crying a lot and
totally losing it on my partner
recently. Is that normal?"

POSTPARTUM DEPRESSION

Postpartum depression is more common than you may know. It can make you feel irritable, angry, guilty, sad, overwhelmed, brain-fogged and isolated. You can completely lose your appetite, or you may eat everything you see. It can even affect your ability to connect with your newborn. You may be unable to sleep, have racing thoughts you can't stop, the list goes on. Please do not be embarrassed or try to hide these feelings. If you think you are going through it, you are not alone. Talk to your partner, your friends, and your family. Ask for help from a therapist or a support group, or go to your doctor to talk about medication. It is very difficult for those that haven't gone through postpartum depression to understand; therefore, finding others who have been there can be extremely validating. Postpartum depression needs validation and acknowledgment so that it can be addressed. Treating it will make for a better you, so you can be better for your baby.

IN THE HOSPITAL AFTER BIRTH

This section is to keep you informed of several tests that need to be done before you leave the hospital. These tests help to ensure your baby is as healthy as can be to go home with you safely. Additionally, I've included explanations of the injection given into the thigh and topical ointment applied to the eyes immediately after birth, as well as the first vaccination.

BILIRUBIN TEST – Elevated levels of bilirubin in the blood are associated with something called jaundice, which is when a newborn's skin and eyes look yellow. However, some newborns can have high levels of bilirubin and not present with jaundice. Therefore, every newborn will get checked before leaving the hospital.

A bilirubin level is checked most often with a device that is placed on the skin without any discomfort to your baby. It provides a close estimation of bilirubin level in the blood. If the number is too high, then a blood specimen (a small pinprick from the heel) must be taken to measure the actual level of bilirubin in the blood. It is important for bilirubin levels to be checked because if elevated levels go undetected, bilirubin can deposit in the brain and cause damage.

If the blood bilirubin level is too high, your baby may need to get phototherapy, aka "blue lights," while they stay in the nursery, usually for twelve to twenty-four hours (sometimes longer). These lights help to reduce the bilirubin level. Frequent feeding also helps, and sometimes formula supplementation will be recommended for breast-fed infants in situations where a mother's milk supply may not have come in yet. Remember, this is supplementing, not substituting. The goal here is to get those bilirubin levels back to normal, so it's ok to supplement for the short term. Formula will not harm and in fact will help.

CCHD (CRITICAL CONGENITAL HEART DISEASE) SCREENING TEST – This test involves wrapping a small piece of tape with an oxygen sensor (aka a pulse oximeter) on one hand and one foot for a few minutes to check your baby's oxygen levels. It is a screening test to detect certain heart abnormalities.

If these levels are concordant, your baby "passes" this test. If the oxygen levels are discordant, then they will need to be further evaluated for a heart defect.

HEARING SCREENING TEST – This will be done to make sure your baby can hear. It is not uncommon for a newborn to have this test repeated a few times before "passing," as amniotic fluid or vernix can remain in the ear canals and alter the results.

Even if you leave the hospital and your baby didn't pass the hearing screen prior to discharge, don't worry, it will be checked again in a few weeks. Less than one percent of newborns actually have true hearing loss.

NEWBORN SCREENING TEST – This test involves a pinprick to your baby's heel to collect some blood to check for very rare, but very serious, diseases that, when caught early, can save their life. The results should be followed up by your pediatrician at one of your first few visits.

VITAMIN K INJECTION – Almost immediately after birth, your baby will receive an injection of vitamin K in the thigh. Vitamin K plays a crucial role in blood clotting. Vitamin K levels are low at birth, so the injection helps to normalize the level to prevent hemorrhagic disease in the newborn. Although rare, hemorrhagic disease can lead to death in the first few weeks of life.

ERYTHROMYCIN EYE OINTMENT – Right after birth, this antibiotic eye ointment will be applied to your baby's eyes. This preventive measure is taken to avoid neonatal conjunctivitis (aka pink eye) due to certain bacteria that may be in the birth canal. Some types of these bacteria, if present, can cause an infection in the eyes that can lead to blindness.

GLUCOSE (SUGAR) LEVEL TESTING – This is necessary for newborns whose mothers have diabetes, for very large and very small newborns, and for preterm and post-term newborns. These groups of newborns are at a higher risk of developing hypoglycemia (low blood sugar). If your newborn does not fall into any of those categories but is showing signs of hypoglycemia, they will be tested as well.

Why is glucose important to monitor? Glucose is the main energy source for all of the organs in the body. If it drops too low for a sustained period of time, it can have repercussions later on with learning and development. Glucose testing is performed by gathering a few drops of blood from the heel.

HEPATITIS B VACCINE – It is recommended that newborns receive their first hepatitis B vaccine within twenty-four hours of birth. Hepatitis B is a viral infection that can lead to liver failure or liver cancer. Symptoms can take years to develop and until they do, infected persons can spread the virus unknowingly. Vaccinating your newborn at birth will help protect them against this debilitating and often fatal disease.